Agitations

and

Allelujas

Agitations

and

Allelujas

Poems

Harvey Steinberg

RAGGED SKY PRESS

PRINCETON, NEW JERSEY

Published by Ragged Sky Press
270 Griggs Drive, Princeton, NJ 08540
www.raggedsky.com

Library of Congress Control Number: 2021953457
ISBN: 978-1-933974-44-6

Cover design by Dirk Rowntree
Cover photo by Harvey Steinberg
This book was designed by Jean Foos and typeset in
    Bodoni URW, Neue Haas Unica Pro and Scala Pro.

Printed in the United States of America

First Edition

To my wife Marcia, for whom love, truth, and fairness are paramount—and she comes with a keen appreciation of humor to balance her formidable serious side. So how can I not persistently *try*? And to my daughters, who, probably unknowingly, continue to teach me to apply proper constraints on myself.

Contents

War: Public and Personal

Here and There

Other Climes, Other Times

Little Folks and Big

Envoi

Introduction: What It's Like to Create Poetry

If a poem never *was*
how do you know what it
could be, or couldn't?
Some things are black and white,
but not *this*, this has hidden in-betweens,
this is like discerning if it's night or day
by twilight.
Which is iffy.
If you put all the poets together
and bunched all the salaried scientists
what might they say?
In one way or another they'd say,
"be prepared for something else."
Me, I'd rather neither prepare
nor not know what's not there.
But I'm stuck, too.

There's no telling the *not* (detail it, I dare you!)
which makes me unsure of the *is*
inasmuch as the *not*, if filled with what *could* be
would probably contain some other kinds of an *is*,
leaving the is you're sure is an is
in a very undesirable state
(like Atlantis, the lost continent).
So what's a fella to do?—
do for decisions like,
"That's that!"
when what's really suspected is,
"What's *this*?"

This is what I'm supplying
so you can hum along with the score
of that grand piece of music,
Beethoven's Tenth Symphony.

The Waywardness
of Love

outside, night retires
more than we can do

The Flood

We're the only ones left,
the Waterfront Wedding awaited us
and now we're near flood tide
the moon is right
the guests have left
so I wait for our official sacred time together
that heretofore was play, or lust, and surely loving,
and looking out the window I remember cutting through the
cool calm waters of a boy-sized lake
arm over arm to the far shore
not far away but far enough, not tried before,
mildly, my shoulders doing the work
timed to my leg kicks;
sequence is no problem for a boy
I remember all parts worked in unison
if not in unison it's when we grew
to plot and be older
as I am now,
planning, or soon to,
soon to memorialize the formal normal deed
in this deluxe resort hotel suite
by this large bay
drowning as I feared I might;
I learned to float and backstroke
topside in air
clouds contoured in pictures above
but in town the backstreets flooded from
the waters gone amuck
the streets adrift where the households took
the rowboats out, knowing what to expect
from the damage done before.

Sarah, will we be ready for what's next
after next?

Quotidian

After six hours sleep
warm to each other's presence,
sun welding in east.

At dawn I scan my face,
shaving like my father
my face beyond mine.

Workday etches illusion,
pretense getting bolder,
becoming what I'm not.

Dusk serves my lips to her cheek.
When words are questionable
be steward of silence.

I was whole all day.
Night, her length informs my length
I was half all day.

At sleep her odors are mine.
Except it might open her eyes,
I'd kiss her closed lids.

Xylem Summers

Trees at age fifteen harbored words,
notions knew nature,
willows framed pastures—
fragments I bring here
to pay dues to fields there
shadowed by arbors in evenings,
a lovelorn young fool
who bayed puppy-love to the moon.

Now remembrance seeks me
seeking stars' omens,
low limbs of apple trees
heavy in August.
Night, I marvel at cold stars;
August, fragrance of fruit trees,
April, blossoms of dogwood.

In your absence
I touch the bark of this tree;
the apple trees weight their branches for you,
the dogwoods do best in mid-shade,
hilltops flourish, hardwoods haunt.

Love's Lastings
An Old-Fashioned Wedding Toast

Assuredly, each to each, with all to all,
astonishments invest you both at first
by voice, form, lilt, light, fragrance,
leaving only taste of lips, and touch,
for further time. As prelude, gestures grip,
and minds fit in tongue and groove companionship.

At this turn, poets usually disclaim all hopes,
speak cleverly, lack patience. Too young,
they warn of boredom, harp on wrinkles, guile,
despair, ungrateful children, temperaments
at odds, lure of drives and lusts, as though
events and time obliterate warm hearts' design.

Poets conceive poets' conceits immortal,
account ironic stanzas as sturdier than life,
plump each discouragement as fatal strife.
While true, that mishaps make for muddle,
directions tangled, reliances and dreams disserved,
still, vows have latency—beyond dreamers' dreams
runs a vein of iron soft as gold
and bright, mined this wedding day, and night.

Divorce

In the Car

 Toward dusk the sky is winter scumbled;
 pink touches down on a transverse streak of yellow.
 I sip its ends and I mouth its center.
 It keeps falling from my lips
 and I drink and drink and drink
 seized fire in ice cubes.

Home

 It's painful to recall the warm hours together.
 Wakefulness licking the mattress,
 retinas eating hues of stocked cupboards,
 our vigorous family in full enactments
 all slip to long-term memory
 whose fire-door sticks.

Love's Losings

Passage of breath before brain stores what's said:
unhampered hints, blood's rush, carouse, hair's tousle,
plenteous meet of mouths, not overtried or denied.
Against the world, flush heart alone was shield,
though, so unguarded, we later dealt
the truth of selves—gestures turned to habit,
platitudes exchanged, false excuse,
resentments, subtle entailments of sly ruse.

When much is gone as though much had not been
and memory lies waste in canceled books
and I in search scrape with broken twig
what mind puts mind to, the branch itself
erasing as it seeks, for courtesy I underwrite
this debt, poeticizing love I half forget.

Calypso Immortal

From Ogygea, Calypso scents the Aegean
with sage, luring Odysseus coastward.
Now his memories sit on the sea
and brine licks at his footfalls.
Ithacan Penelope, too, ankles in frothtide,
paces to quicken her heart which wildly beats
and in turn numbly slows, destitute and deranged.
Calypso will not retire, not deny guilt
nor offend chasteness, they are one,
desire and distancing
no less or more divisible
than sets the sea-god roaring, Poseidon
blinded in his churning sea-spray,
hurt, needful of mortals as mortals of him,
the paradox.
This ocean is endless until it ends,
until the winds sough, gust again,
a raft built, the Greek on his way,
and fidelity find reward
as Calypso quietly tends to her sumptuous garden
and sends for old lovers.

Orpheus and Eurydice Unexplained

What the reasons, scholars debate.

It was his own sweet music drove him on,
wind ruffling waves, rustlings of wheat:
Orpheus who strung his Thracian lyre
to charm serpent and sedgewort, their very rocks;
yet Eurydice was lost to his love when too early he turned
his attention toward her.
It's never been known why he erred
in defying the caution, why, although warned,
he cast their hopes toward disaster,
precluding safe passage of his stolen betrothed.
He broke the arbitrary but not ambiguous rule
and pays with her absence from him,
he from her, an eternal mutual emptiness,
returned as she is to dark chambers of deep.

Pity them, while scholars prate.

Poconos Tryst

(After Shakespeare's Sonnet 29,
"When in disgrace with fortune and men's eyes")

When on this heart-shaped bed that's undersized
I all alone stretch forth my bootless feet,
shivering post-hot-tub as my body dries
and look upon these toes and scratch my seat
thinking of thee in beauteous choirs and tropes
like Shakespeare in his footed sonnets blessed,
we both with Athlete's Foot and dismal mopes,
myself with hotel fare contented least;
in turbid state I find myself perspiring
as gastric acids sour the custard tarts I ate—
then, in my nakedness you apprising
these stringy limbs, this belly that's a crate—
  Should you the fungicide and towel bring,
  my Itch would be for you alone and dry for you my Thing.

Fixing Her Wagon

(After Shakespeare's Sonnet 18,
"Shall I compare thee to a summer's day?")

Shall I compare thee to a tinker's dray?
Thou art more broad-beamed and less sensibly ornate.
Bronz'd cowbells that doth swing doth say
the services they vaunt are far more delicate
than your misguided taste you think divine:
thy Easter bonnet seen immensely-brimmed
sets off, for common view, a vacant mind
from which tresses flow by stylists trimmed
to flagrant flaunt the hair you've purple dyed
in Clairol's promise worthy of its boast
while nothing that I do can turn your tide
of red-ink oceans washing up my coast.
  So long as mind can seethe at female sham
  there's nothing for it but a tinker's damn.

Sculptures at the Met

Obstetricians (for whom nudity is tedium),
convening, tour the Metropolitan Museum.
Unused to looking up instead of down
(their procedure once they don the gown)
incredulously view a stone sylph's vertical position
and try to comprehend this anatomically odd condition.
Recovering, they in conclave give their nod of recognition
to what they comprehend through obstetrical cognition:

I'M TALKING BELLY BUTTONS!

They counted belly-buttoned statues in profusion,
seventeen times more innies than protrusions
which our physicians in scientific exultations
proclaimed, is "quite the innie/outie ratio among our patients
and reflects the National Institute of Health's statistic;"
until . . . until at statuesque Athena they go ballistic!

I'M TALKING BELLY BUTTONS!
BY ZEUS, ATHENA HAD NONE!

In dire confabulation they stake their reputations on this peg:

"SHE MUST HAVE BEEN AN EGG!"

At Grecian myths I incline toward distress,
the idea there being, "miraculously impress;"
so it's not for long I'll further pull your leg:
there is no question here of any egg,
or what Merck's Manual may have said,
for

ATHENA SPRANG WHOLE FROM ZEUS'S HEAD!

One young physician reeled vertiginous
as Athena's middle made him more than middling amorous;
he disgraced himself forever, ruled the Medical Board
when, on his tour within the female ward
he wandered in search of women without a natal cord.

Four Quickies

Oh happy thought! That
snakes slither bellies over
each other! We too!

~~~~~~~

Our bodies in bed
where everything's a lever
for everything else.

~~~~~~~

She was Irish, b'gosh and b'gorra,
he was Jewish, kine-ahora;*
his ecumenical habits
were so like that of rabbits
that Jehovah turned him Angora.

~~~~~~~

Rome's rotund basso profundo
couldn't sing "voice over," just under
his diva soprano
fought him mano a mano
as he roamed her bottom rotunda.

*Recited to ward off the Evil Eye

Stepping Outdoors

pre-dawn awakeness
generates Haiku 'til six
the river ripples ~~~~

A Boy's September Catskill

A spectral pleasure crests in every cell
glorifying sting
his bloodied knee
peroxide steeps,
sacramental
as hissing pond
hymns daysong.
The boy chants lips to
fall's sienna flask,
of earths blown;
touches knee's suppuration,
plasma sun splashing blood flares.

Autumn night slabs its goldened marble
reddish crimson-black black. Black.
The youth reclining on the chilly porch
is phosphorescent raptor of the skies
encased in comets' five thousand blinking owlish eyes.
Mother's rhinestones on her fancy dress, do not touch
they'll
fall.
In his hand, the porch too dark to see,
a yellow-carmine flake of skin he's peeled;
just below the scrape,
the purple-black contusion where the leg hit stone.

The stars stay fast.
                    He fingers them.

Dour Journey

Glued by gravity in thrusting Ford on dipping road,
in multiple dimensions of mind
rambling through suburban swards
toward river habitats again, the water band flows south
incising fifty sudden years ago.

The deep well of time remits its substance pail by pail.
Skewed plats of grainfields possessing as possessed
invade a farmer's sweetest dreams season after season after season;
morning after morning dew-beaded stalks, like music's signatures,
confirm the rhythms of the day to follow
until, unbidden—contemptuous of all that went before—
the word *finis* trails out.

Destiny, not years alone,
transits to this white compelling holding page
tough as caustic gauze tightened on
a stiff-hipped flesh-drawn farmer's 1950s' economic ache that
clamped his bones but not his reverence,
frayed his wife's conceits but not her Sabbath morning
pure-voiced singing.

Now suburbia spreads its ivy patches green as clover crop,
azalea where alfalfa plumed; pink begonia blooms
accessorize a mammoth plastic daisy;
beyond the shoulder's culvert ditch past verge,
sedge-hid and weather scoured,
a battered aged softball's twine intestines leak.

Barren claims of farm exemption edge this day.
Aging memory draws taut on either side
straight across where road descends
refracting woken dawn river's moist mouth,
a kiss blown
a semi-young man's semi-old man's
windscored cheek.

Bright Day

Stepping out
to morning's sharp porch
split by sunlight,
this eager skin:

mind half made up,
one eye cocked,
rail fence reeling,
crows calling,
       calling,
         cawling.

An Aesthete Takes the World As It Is

Meant to actuate, its blue chill fastened me:
the ten-foot joggers' arrow painted on the grass
parched my winter morning's walk
across the stubbled reservation tinted with
the light of Sunday grace and heady wakefulness.

Blithe music wasn't there for the listening, or solemnity:
solace waited afar in the outstretched fields
unlimited in their telling as they tendered peaceable
communions, what's unheard beyond
the seeds drowsing and the bugs that wait for spring.

The blue graffiti stunned the park's protocols;
unease is a panther behind my chair as I ruminate.
I do confess the incautious spur
of perfectly nice people disquieting green
astonishes my paintings in the slash of my brush.

I have no psalm to sing, and mercy's uncertain.

Patio Lunch at Sculpture Gardens

Monet behind the flowers
he might have been another year,
a hundred years and more before:
the gentleman who sits there now munching,
vines behind and lady like a cameo beside,
his jacket open, his chat intent
on what was and what will be,
velvet murmurs.

Through the arch, rearing up the hillocks
across the bridge above a lily pond,
glyphs of stone, brass, steel, composite, glass,
which muse and muscle of their founders goad to life
conjoin all who pass and go.
But Oh!
Monet lifts Samsung phone to ear,
his throat extruding out metallic spears.
I steel myself for what I am
within my time and scope
bent over Molson Ale and Chicken Wrap
and a take-out box for storing Monet's lilies.

Cat Visit—Lawrenceville

Kinetic cat slips down abdomen to earth,
her only business now the exit
imperceptible to human eye.

A tennis ball sticks beneath the chain-link barrier
she scrapes under, into the Volvo car lot.

Trots on lightly;
black orange white, tan-tufted cheek,
sucking in distances.

Cat that licks your hand eludes you,
good-will gone at tongue-done time,
job completed; palm sanded,
sealed with varnish.

Is that her tail switching in a timothy brake
beside the brigade of Volvos?
Perhaps it's an item on newsprint
flapping in the wind.

Shadow-plays among the sun-plunged cars mark her hunt.
Or are they shimmers of my languor
as I watch her out my window?

Some Rules and Regulations Re: Felines

Do not pin a name on him, lest you presume.
Formulate intents when you quest the cat.

In tracking him you will be deceived;
your own failings will stalk you.
He will turn his head to stare back
in survivable ways to which you have no permit.

If you set him on fire or drown him
you will know fire and drowning;
you will know yourself more sharply
the older you get.

I know, I have done it,
or dreamt I've done it.

I have chewed the charred and matted fur
and cried how time has choked me.

Do not ask of him.
His jealous kin will come from around the corner.
You will have to pay them back by telling
what you do not want
yourself
to know.

Tapestry of Night Hounds

Moon dogs sigh, snuffle, doze;
soon their hunter's moon will bloom,
their silent scents invest in Kingdom room
a blood-pool panting.
At sundown by the golden dome
a drowsing hound flops its head in waiting,
baited for the silvery disc
part-risen to drag its drugging tide
around the canine's dormant, quivering hide.
Raked by ink-smudged sky: the Moon,
Orion nebula, veiled Milky Way outspread,
perhaps metastasis,
the willy-nilly inevitably coming
to claim the spellbound hounds'
stalking night adventures.

The moon has slyness,
connives to slip its sullen rays silently away
anticipating day when white sun's sails furled, unfurl,
flay open subtle night to frights of day
which daze the moondogs' haze of indigo;
sun's rising not the whimper in a dream
but a wakened scream obliterating pale light
nightly fugitively seen.
Earlier, when dusk, a waiting;
stars' lights recessed in atmospheric fog
receiving, reflecting sweep of moonmist,
stones, mute gates,
Kingdom where hounds bed down,
fraternize with dreams
in hunt dementia.

~~~~~~~~

the sweet glades are gone,
and the grainfields
succeeding
are succulent too

Writer's Quest

Art is taking risks.
It's about jumping off cliffs
onto thin paper.

Hemingway

As I sit my rump presses down
which propels something inchoate up to my head
to swiftly descend to my pen and evolve onto paper.
My ass is flat getting flatter and it's a Wonder,
but then again Hemingway's was round while he wrote
I do believe
and he wrote
standing
up.
I'm too damn limp to be an upstanding guy
and he was a stand-up guy who was sad
he couldn't protect the Old Man of the Sea.
You know the rest of the story, he killed him off.
It always made me sad.
Papa shot himself through the mouth
when he had too much of enough of himself.
He could've shot off a toe. That's what I'd do in his shoes,
i.e., to be accurate, *out* of them.
So I'll sit here and I won't be acclaimed.
I'll write for readers who don't like the ellipses
they're supposed to fill up in Hemingway's stories
with fillips of their own savage imaginings.
I wouldn't shoot myself so raw my jaw falls out—
in prevention of which I may never get off my ass.
For literary effect, I'll ask,
"What does one sit on *but* one's ass?"
Try feet first, hands down, chests out,
arms akimbo, fists balled, chins up,
they're not for sitting on, only the ass,
except, from what I've experienced,
the ass doesn't know how to connect them all
like Hemingway did,
who, when he couldn't rise to the occasion any longer,
put himself down.

Of Emily Dickinson

A flower poked its face at me—
tiny as it was,
it magnified my wonderment
more than learning does.

A teacher poked his face at me—
craggy as it seemed,
it showed me bridges I must cross
to ways I had not dreamed.

A spirit poked its face at me—
features I could not tell,
that put to question what I was
in this corporeal shell.

Overload

I bite off a chunk of learning
that's next to Everything, yet I'm yearning.

My books rattle on the shelves.

The genius of a book
is lit by a thousand thousand nuances
quivering next to the next book on the shelf
—culled from some forgotten place—
containing supernova in its nanospace.

I download texts from Papyrus-In-Print
up through eBay dot com,
hard-copy all messages onto my sheets
(plus the fizzy gists between lines),
count the letters one by one on a sheet,
multiply them by the sheets in the stack
by reprints on the rack
by . . .

Does this immensity
mean, "Read all the volumes,"
or signal: "Don't try"?

Does this say I'm a homunculus
too scant to be scanned?
What is the plot?
Am I an "I,"
or not?

William Carlos Williams

Have you, as I, contemplated
that what is true and tough and unbreakable
about W.C. Williams is, it's
hard to burrow your way into *Paterson*,
or out?

Unashamedly, I can't parse what he writes at times
except it feels valid
except it's got the pull of a mule
except it's authentic
(sometimes, he says, the unlikely expressions of everyday speech)
and I thank W.C.W.
but I miss—
ah me, I miss—
the music,
whoever may say they hear it.

It's hard to confess this.
I'll be looked askance at critique sessions,
my library card will be forfeit.

Near sixty years dead yet Will's still alive
and I have to argue with his kith and kin
and the academies he despised
and myself too!

Address by a Hot Poet to a Cool 'Un

You say: Four-alarmers are indelicate,
they are not susceptible to nuances,
distendable as rhythms.
They are too big,
too rough,
too red.

Fires don't mean anything, you say.

I could tell you about them all day and all night,
read you the records,
take you to The Towering Inferno picture-show six times,
blow hot till your face goes pizza,
blow fire-sirens till your nose caves in from sound waves
or buy you sonar to pick up sizzles a thousand miles away.

You'd say, "Wails don't count,
you can't use them as voice,
fires aren't *there*,
cool it,
they don't mean anything."

I get your point.

Here's *mine*:
Get me out of this burning building!

~~~~~~~~

Oh Lord, tame this brute!
Unfurl his tongue!
Provide vocabulary!

War:
Public and Personal

In this stout country
why is it alright to say
I'm often wary?

An Overheard War

This java's just what I was looking for,
you know? The boring slow ride up the parkway?
Ah yes, rush-hour can be such a nuisance,
systole and diastole hooked to each push of the brake;
then, ho-hum, unwrapping burgers at the cholesterol rest stop
judiciously spreading barbecue sauce
across TV's subaudible hum of the off-somewhere war
where it seems there are shrouds and obsessions
acted out with *plastique* fashioned somewhere.

I believe I forget places, my own face, I'm not sure.
In my pockets I carry the traces to tell me:
keys for the Ford to go
plus the laundry list of cash, cards,
tissues, spiral notebook, Pilot Pen,
the Book of Life
the names of all men
and the bottomless wail.

War Zone

You were meant to be taken devoutly.
You cared to be part of something.
I was prayerful too.
Now you are in want of consolation.
I make the agonized howl
you had no time to form.

Breath molds on my lungs.
I walk by candlelight.
You were used to my ramblings,
I was the friend on your tongue,
we flocked across a held moon.

What should the memory-hunter do?
How should the archeologist tag it?
Who's the lad in charge?
In what time, location, and circumstance
were we held firm by each other?

A padding past my hallway—
something moves.
Who comes across it?

Candlelight, the mourners sob and cry.
The face featured just so, the remains waxen,
with left side and right,
each appendage of similar length;
ankles partnering each other,
the nails of left and right identifiably alike.
All is there, yet you're not.

The harvest of that plain
fed the hungers of war
as the moon plunged into a chasm.
Oh, this saying Yes for generous limbs
that hold friends holy!

I Say the Night

I say the night has bears in it,
pack wolves, and other lurkings of the heart
whose prowls give way
to pleasantries of day—
yet in this heart of darkness stay.

And That's That!

Death denies man's immortal and, while living,
men counsel a course to allay the dread.
One shouts, "Hurry to compact the case you're making,"
another slurs, "Slow down if you'd race against death."
No avail: Hades takes all whatever the plea.
The aberrations men bring are called their "Free Will,"
what they believed in when the gods weren't looking;
you'd think there's a third path not so perverse.
Maybe that's why they end up resigned to Hades,
however they study their course they're lost at the last.
Making up one's own mind?! Hardly!
Don't you know of the two sets of ledgers,
one in men's hands and one Hades keeps open
near a forge in the great hall of his kingdom?

> *I ask me about me, is life a dream?*
> *Where does it come from, where does it go?*
> *Who is there in it, who does what's been done?*
> *Is there a song in it, is there a hearer?*
> *Is this a baptism, is this a dirge?*

Ask Hades: What worth is the underworld for?
His hiss: "For your knees to the floor!"

Memorial Day

Thoughts etch the crusted soil Generals speak to.
The earth heaves, separates, layers over.

Pre-dawn awakeness, the nearby river ripples.
They would tear their cerements,
lurch and linger.

Through green fields coursing, river seals the earth.
Who caresses their brows?

Cyclops

Day fades;
more than the bastard
of sea-stormed Poseidon,
one-eyed brute Polyphemus
the Cyclops
can do.

Mired in rank entrails,
sun downing
and torchlights rising,
Polyphemus tears at his kill,
skulls flung nearby
to the execrable pile.

Moon's conjuring light
breeds lunacy.
Night, dreams flaming,
Cyclops lays waste with thousand eyes
and in single sight wakes

VORACIOUS

~~~~~~~~

the bed talking back
the bad dreams conflagrating
Mother's tirades soon

Here and There

heart bursting at both,
a stream through green banks coursing,
mid-town outpouring

The Sunday Travel Section

Am I lost in longings? "Triumphal arches
mark where Caesar's boots crossed to glory
there," declaims the tourist scribe, whose story
rallies me to join the lines of march.
"Shun domestic prattle! New Jersey shores depart
whose cottages sift sand; touch the quarried
blocks piled by doting ancients! Crete
four hundred decades gone out-towers Walmart."

The Sunday morning coffee perks, roots me
to the breakfast chair as grandson's food
defaces all the stories fit to print.
Unlike exalting columns, my past boots me
to everlasting reprint, forever rude
reminder that daily life is lifelong stint.

Next Stop Next

Cocktail time—
At the Cozy Time Inn
they spoke of
they explained
they paid
for on-the-rocks and edibles
and their pro-rata share of the Cozy Time mortgage.
I spent my money just like everyone else.
The room canted dizzy
as the chatter went cozy.
One ol' gal from Texas had her elbow on
The Geology of Love
she'd bought at the Hard Rock Bookstore
and to de-map my sweetheart at home
she displayed her own atlas with
Astounding Mountains across double sheets.

Her atlas showed International Sights and Prize Winners
with soaring Swiss Bridges
and how I
got stranded on an ascending girder
hundreds of feet in the air
through a telephoto lens
which sucked me in close
via a barrel
then blasted me out at her feet
like a flying squirrel goes splat
and bungling again I submitted,
so drawn to her volumes of Physical Science
as she sent me spinning
that as best I could study it out
electrons become ions
and then reattach
elsewhere.

Crossing 7th Avenue

Minimalist pop, he pop-a-dopped
as he popped past,
bounding across the wrigley wrapper
whitely crumpled in the gutter crevice
the paper sheath perched on a soot mound
ravaged of its minty juices.
Shrived by morning light
like PUREFAITH
its brilliance staked a momentary claim
on Cal's distress.

Pop-a-dop
a modernist fop,
guttersnipe gum ge-bragh! gesacht Cal.
No sweat, a virginal start again
if I make it to the sidewalk
"until I meet the next peril"
Cal's set of mind was
optimize
minimalist
pop.

POP!

Jersey Shore

crystalline sky
her child eyes

~ ~ ~ ~ ~ ~ ~

Honeymoon
beach chairs
empty

~ ~ ~ ~ ~ ~ ~

attention on sandpipers
as lunch flies away ~ ~ ~
gulled again

Einstein and Me

In Princeton
where Einstein
for thirty years
failed to extract
from God's cosmos
the unified field
I whip my egg for lunch
and strive in vain
to spoon up
from the bowl
a white crisp of shell.

New Orleans Parish

Where sundowned lawn to river flows
solitary folk descend.
At a farther esplanade
hotel chatter pricks a caustic sky
gusting gulls to swing away
and arc return
through nightshow's indigo divide.
A naval vessel stays itself,
tethered as a resting hound.
On Saturday casual night-watch
amid the deck's mad machinery
sailors hunt unguarded memories,
murmurs of their dreams
half-said half-heard among themselves
double-shadowed by crossed lamps.

From 11 to 4 on Sunday
tourists board the minesweeper
in Woldenberg Park.
Emboldened by Saturday night leave
a still-boyish ensign fields questions
as he cocks his white cap toward the Gulf.
    A grandmother questions, "Do you get cold at sea?"
      "We button our jackets," he makes her feel warm.
    A father inquires, "Is it dangerous work?"
      "We're trained, so no sweat," he wants him to think.
    A teen-ager probes, "How far down do mines go?"
      "Deep as my kiss of last night," he reels in the boy.

The Circle

It's all guesswork, what I'll do now
I don't know why we can't all be nice for now
there's enough murder in the works without
splattering crimson on this sheet
I think.
I've just had breakfast and now
is to decide what to do
on Sunday *my* day
for exercise and athletics and boom-de-boom-boom
and I don't even know what I mean by boom-de-boom-boom
I hope I find out
I'm sort of going around in circles
trying to keep things simple
circling myself for a straight answer
to the strange and bizarre and loopy ways of mankind
and womankind *with* mankind
(I can't help but shy at how macho I've put this)
and it has me in a tizzy
at my head going 'round like a
high-wheel bicycle
of olden days sometimes I'm the small
wheel sometimes I'm the big
but in any case if it goes over it's one hell of a fall
so bicycles were invented so feet
touched the ground
if they had to
or if it was wise to
and they're touching the ground now
but so what, I'm stopped!
So what? So other bikers come along and
they say "What's the matter?" and
I reply, "I don't know where I want to go" and
they all gather around

me in a circle mingling and they come up with
"We're your circle of friends" and
"We'll help you decide" and
"There's a rink or a track or a velodrome
 call it what you will (if you would)
 the other side of this megalopolis
 but we can find it and tame the distance and
 the uncertainty of its location and
 we'll go around with you so if you fall off your bike
 we'll be there for you
 it's a peculiar track
 there are gradients and potholes
 and bad food at stations alongside
 but we've doctors will fix you up if you fall
 (*when* you fall) and you'd like to rise
 like the Savior at Easter and
 won't you be glad you've got spirit
 unless you don't believe
 but that's OK
 it works for agnostics and atheists too"
 is what I hope they'll say
"and before you know it you'll be
 in the circular path with us where
 at every station we go 'round
 you come back to yourself and
 you're able to write a poem
 about your well-grounded well-rounded
 balance in this crazy world
 and that for you, friend,
 is what's meant by
 boom-de-boom-boom."

~~~~~~~~

moon strung over sea

breaks at esplanade's footings

rowboats . . sea . . . moonstones!

Other Climes, Other Times

Ever so many
less killed than in Viet Nam
was the Bay of Pigs.

Gdańsk is a seaport city in Poland that was oppressively ruled by the Soviet Union and its Polish minions. In 1980 workers struck the shipyard, a first step in freeing Poland from Soviet dominion. The rebellion is commonly called "Gdańsk."

Poland before Gdańsk: 1

Out there is a pulpy ear.
Perhaps.
Perhaps it's a cloud engulfed,
the Devil peeing on his sulfur coal
at Krakow Gasification Plant #2.
Perhaps this poem goes nowhere
because I don't know who I'm addressing.

My mouth is stuck inside my cerebrum,
a vault with painted saints
but no vents,
without rookery to fly my message to the front.
It sweats my patience
that only tiny husks of wheat remain in place.

A Soul somewhere,
but right smack on this mark
the split of mind and body speaks for a corpse
huffing under the landing.

"I die, that's how I know I've been,"
said Descartes in finality,
his vocal cords locking up,
and outside, no ear, finally.

Poland before Gdańsk: 2

When vanguard shadows of endless armies of fear
troop the unlit room, and householders slump
worn out limbs within the gloom, thick fingers
clench. Within that fist white palms
keep holy winter-Poland's homeland snow
of warm memories reclaimed.

                    Bread and steel fire in Polish crucibles!

To the invader's lunging stench
the slit with feminine scent near belly and thigh
checks massive plunge; clinched womb repels
to wait for birth of Poland's make,
simmered in honey and steeped in the sacred bowl.

                    Against alien hold, a thousand years
                    of progeny fire in Polish crucibles!

Smug proclamations sweep the crowd herded
to cover, a shivering fox grounded by dogs.
As K-9 cops blast whistles, round nuns
shopping intermittently at smoky market stalls
shush the hounds and inch up eyes in peace to
pray:

                    "Mother Mary, may more than chestnuts
                    fire in Polish crucibles!"

~~~~~~~~

in the heat of bloom
Mount Fuji shivers

China

the billion cells
of a single linden leaf
flutter with the leaf

A Woman's Ghost Story

Vaporous and twisting he visits
when I sleep.
Days too when called on.
Spirits can be fierce or quiet.
Sleeping, he invests me; waking too
he stirs my yin we do not consummate.
Sometimes I don't know sleeping from waking
as dawn birdchirps nettle me.

My ancestor dances a ghost brush
across generations, his agile paintings;
or else he moves my hand unmannered
as my feet are indelicate.
Each mark I stare at I cannot read.
When no one is looking
I stroke my children's raven hair.

Sharp mountains slant above our valley.
Waters stream the village
to slide under the cottage;
white birds skivvy in.
Spectres who left bones well-ordered
mingle barbarically, chalk-motes over the water.

Father's mother's father I depend on,
not my husband Ch'ang Fu's surly family,
his mother's ghost who plagues me.
I have my father's ancestor chase her out.
I would have him clear Ch'ang Fu's breath
of feathers of beer when he wakes for more.

My ancestor is banded to me
but he does not set peach liquor at my feet.
Our family's wealth are Ch'ang Fu's breath and my feet;
his deters bill collectors, my peasant feet daunt amorous lords.

When I pick at my bunions, not even husband
takes excessive pleasures with me.

Ancestor's cloak writhes.
I say my feet are good for walking,
I can squat to dress my children,
my flat soles crush bugs on the house floor.
Brigands will not carry me off.
Surely if one comes from the west
he wants women with broken arches, undercurled toes.

Though I want my ancestor to stay, his shroud
swims distant and near as sea on a scroll,
a gray cliff behind
and here a great jade peacock.
If this story survives, he wrote it,
or moved this peasant's hand.

Ch'ang Fu would scowl and keep rice from me.
Husbands do not hold spirits as a wife must.

Fine Liquor of Philosophy

Fragile plum-skin ornaments its pulp:
inside, the pit keeps
hard, centered, impervious
to bruises and worm-breakfasts.

At the tavern of plum-wine, sips
of "turned fruit" thin memories of home,
my face so deep in the cup
I can't hear shaking boards and voices nearby.

It's my choice, isn't it,
to stop thinking big about nothing, to join
cronies cultivating laughter,
to put my small seed among theirs?

I will go to Chen and say,
"Your second son wore a costly blue sash yesterday;
how did he get so wealthy?"
I don't have to ask this question, but I do,
I want to prick Chen's false modesty.

Is my insistent mingling a keepsake of the Way?

In the corner, a keg of plum-wine holds the answer.

My Master the Authority

Thinking pains my back.
Beaten,
red auras surround the bamboo's
stripes laid on me by
Master's brushstrokes.

If he will write
on me, I don't mind,
a surface must be ready to his hand.

My Authority huffs, "To be beaten
is to ask to be beaten,"
as his flail weakens.
"I know,
beat me again," I respond,
"do not tire of your taking.
I am poor.
With whom else can I exchange philosophies?"

Elders tell me
not to think so much,
"follow the Way."

Now when I enter his garden
to clip a crimson rose
my Authority turns his own back
which aches from applying the switch.
See, my own flowers
beside his bamboo grove.

How many perfections has the Way.

In the Harbor

See how it's pleasant
to be safe.
Sampans crease the shallows
and a junk slowly drifts to shore.
Fishermen fold their nets.

Sea-bass are not at their usual depth today.
Traveling in, sailors sponge
their eyes without speaking,
husbanding what they missed, deviling risk.
The dice on blanket
tumble, roll, reposition fortune.
For Lo Ping, the jar at home will be lighter by tomorrow,
coins will not rise to the top,
the women will whisper.

Another morning white crests flew,
torsos bent and were slammed to the mast,
eyes blind from salt spray.

These are the waters,
broken yesterday and becalmed today.

Blessings come alone, troubles together.

Lost and Found

When I turn earth to where I came from,
digging for the roots of ancestry
I find a shallow grave that tests me—
one scant generation past, which casts me dumb.
I strain to hear the voices that don't come
past parents' chants which hailed me
as the next in progeny, yet muted
their past numbers, leaving me a slender sum.

Like friends, I found my footing in the city schoolyard
where I stubbed a toe against the concrete crack
in rounding first; to reach home's hard
but hopeful; better or worse, I acquired the knack
to run my own circuit without tracking others',
face to the wind, not looking back.

Tickets Taken with Dad

"Hustle up, kid!" Pop calls at me over his shoulder.

Outflanking the attendant's zealous hand
by a deft and natural move,
Pop's nicotined fingers
sweep atop the glass-sided box
delivering into it the two tickets
which prink, grin, and wheeze
atop the others already there,
the last ones in
before the planetarium show starts.

I hustle beneath the pseudo-firmament
where the zodiac is not more illusionist than Pop
unwrapping the world to his concoction
as backs of seats slanted
with our shanks pushing forward
Sagittarius streaks its light to the dome.

"Maybe stars are really holes in the sky," Pa tests,
"and cosmos the inside of an eggshell."

I sign on, content with his whimsy.

Or, half-price Wednesday nights of the B-movie "stinkers"
at the Commodore movie palace right by the El;
maybe a seafaring flick with castaways
flushing through waters toward tinctures of landform,
knowing only drift, pea-soup shroud
thickened by Pa's Pall Mall addiction:
journeyers grasping thin spars.
Sometimes, crinoline romances in old New Orleans
setting off jokes in the balconies
like handballs a thousand times
slapped against a wall,

palpable for a while,
then laid by.

Pa passed up my report cards without looking.
I wrote out his birthday cards with care.

When my job moved to Jersey he wouldn't come to visit;
he needed transcendence,
Miami, the magical boat ride that circles Manhattan
(Manahatta he called it, like Whitman),
or even the ferry to Staten Island—
so long as it wasn't New Jersey.

"But I'm closer and less time than Miami," I persisted.
"That may be so," he said, "but not *Tampa*."

I could have struck him
except that he loved my kids and my wife and me too
although he wouldn't visit.

He added (discerning while not accepting my hurt),
"Listen, with one token and passes
I can make my way to every world culture
right here in New York. Chinese, even Manchurian."

"So why are you leaving for *Tampa*?!" I screeched.

"The waterfront. I'll send you back a herring."

"You know it's more than a thousand miles
to the West Coast of Florida?!
And herring don't inhabit the Gulf?!"

"Could be," he pitied me.

I had unwisely plunged into his fabulary
where, performing his backstroke,
he conjured up fish.
"Write," he ordered, or asked.
"I bought my ticket.

I'll drop you a line.
And take care of your mother,
I won't be around."

I received in the mail a card greeting, "Dear Family—
I'm on a waterfront bench. Just met a handsome
young couple here with a brindle boxer dog
with three heads. His name is Cerberus.
The fishermen are catching everything out of sight.
Love, Dad"

I jotted back a letter
excessively about my daughters
to make him plead guilty.
I signed it effusively large, "YOUR SON,"
then P.S.ed, "What about the herrings?"

"Never bet against a sure thing,"
he replied on a photo postcard that showed a huge sailfish
hung by his tail at a contest weigh-station,
at its side some idiot in galoshes
beside the dead fish-eyes,
vacantly staring into the lens.

That was the last of that.

Dad kept a note-pad before he passed.
"High Times," it was called,
manufactured in Hong Kong,
"80 sheets 5 inches by 3."
On its cover, two innocent flower kids
sheltered under a tree,
a he and a she
clinging to love.
I write these iconic lines
projecting Dad's visions of himself with his bride
westering, pioneering a new age.
And they did.

They sailed on their 1928 prairie schooner
right into the Great Depression.

Anyway, on that pad after Mom died
lay the ghosts of his dreams
setting up ghosts for me.
Entry: "April 4. Cinema 1. 'Nasty Habits.' N.G."
Entry: "April 6. The Beekman. 'Slap Shot.' Good."
Entry: "April 25. Baron. 'Annie Hall.' O.K."
Entry: "Sunday, May 1. Harvey Here."

After my soul snagged on his doorstep
at Lincoln Co-op in Brooklyn,
after composing my fury and love and despairs,
after kissing his cheek,
hand touching his shoulder,
surreptitiously scanning the rooms
to check their deportment for signs of morale
Dad announced, "Harve, I've got a new ticket!"

I deceptively cheered, "Let me see!"

He laid his cards out:

Century Theatres Movie Club for Senior Citizens (*yellow* card)
Associated Independent Theatres Senior Citizens Movie Club (*pink*)
RKO Stanley Warner Golden Age Senior Club (*gold*)
Cinema 5 Theatres Senior Citizens Pass (*ivory*)
UA Senior Citizens Movie Card (*canary*)
Walter Reade Organization Senior Citizen Discount Card (*buff*)

plus red, blue, whatever,
a phantasmagoria
missing the clincher
he held in his hand,
the all-everything card
that trumped
downtown cops,

loan sharks,
horses that quit,
loneliness,
social discomfort,
high blood pressure,
Greyhound buses he had run out of gas for,
and myself who behaved badly.

For his widower's game of solitaire
Pop acquired a joker for spice,
a wild card mustard-hued
to boost him to "sky's the limit,"
Aladdin's carpet for make-believe land
that proved harder to board every month:
"THE GOLDEN AGE MOVIE CLUB"
enabling
"DISCOUNT ADMISSION AT ALL THEATRES
DISPLAYING THIS EMBLEM"
—the Emblem a woman's and man's head
joined in occipital regions
with profiles facing outward
in opposite directions
each seeking
the palace of Oz.

"Member 4376," I read. "That's not bad."
"I got it as soon as I could," Dad answered.
"Do me a favor, Harve, print my name in the box."

The letters formed themselves of birthright
carved on ancestral stone hewn from Masada.
I felt useful. Finally, he'd called on me.
Blood suffused ink as I wrote.

Later that year, or the next,
"High Times" read
Entry: "July 17. Home. Library. Rain."

Entry: "July 18. Mt. Sinai Hospital. Greenwich Village."
Entry: "July 19. Battery Park."
Entry: "July 20. Helene's Birthday yesterday."
Entry: "July 21. Brighton Beach."
Yet later, "Fell. Hurt Back."
Then weekly "Mt. Sinai"
commingled with
Movies and
Race Tracks and
Trips and
the word "Surgery";
EKGs, X-Rays, G.I.'s,
Bone Scans,
Prescriptions—
until his move to my sister in Maryland.

The first—and last—we knew were the growths.

He'd been wrecked badly before.
Left eye outed by a BB,
driver's license forever revoked
(a falling out with a downtown cop),
back broken by gravity
(the fall of a massive machine on him),
finger severed by rotation
(the bread-slicer was eccentric, he noted),
and so on and so forth.
Just the usual for that time and place.
He'd been blind-sided:
burned as a chef,
concussed (a jutting beam at Jamaica Race Track),
punctured (his baling hook took him,
tons of cartons he'd stabbed
in cahoots with his hook, he opined).
Once he went up in flame
from his cigarette ash

that lit on a blue bathrobe I'd bought him
for Chanukah before fire-retardant days.
Holding the charred remnant Pop stood naked
to ask, "You've got a receipt to return this?"

I'd hold my breath as he'd squeeze out his glass eye,
or girdle his back and truss his rupture
concealed by his clothes,
or produce his invisible fingertip
we always forgot was not there
because, you know,
he was a shaman.

For my boyhood invite
to the riddles of Being,
Pop gave me a pass to that show.
The obnoxious fungus that grew from his body
sprouted excitement at Mount Sinai;
interns circled about Dad,
white robes fronting blue frocks of Professors
till Dad was . . . well, was like hidden by cumulus clouds
within azure Heaven
waiting for angels to show up.
The nether world called instead.

Pa wasn't devout but he preferred
being yearly inscribed in the Book of Life
for the year ahead.

At Suburban Hospital in Bethesda
he asked me for that,
for I was my father's son
and although I'd been stunned by his games
I knew his sincerities.

Toward the last, when he said,
"I'll be going. Have them write me a ticket,"
I presumed I'd caught on.

"To Tampa?"
"Sure, don't worry your head.
 I've fed Cerberus, all his three gullets.
 With one very large herring.
 You're learning," he warranted.
"When the bus comes sign me on."
 Then he lifted his shades and winked his good eye
 as the pitted one, turning red,
 terrified me.

~~~~~~~~

it's all up in the air
so far as I can see
this crane-dancing city

Little Folks and Big

frocked girls:
morning glories,
poems in petals

A.D.H.D.

Touched lightly, as a feather his thought flew.
We brooded, "What are he and we to do?"
Our boy could read but couldn't stop stopping.
He'd dash about failing direction, or
(in a hard case metaphors are so artificial,
the gloss over what can't be denied)—
if you will, he couldn't swim the waters to landfall.
We, lost at his losses, his truncated speech,
movements flicked not *at* us, but regardless *of* us,
his five-second brilliance impregnable, so it seemed,
to what he'd said, or will say, or wants to;
the boy's angel smile creasing his face.
We asked ourselves, quietly each other in corners,
"Is he impervious; why can't we communicate?"
Quickly! quickly! his attention span shrinking,
his fineness, his kindness to us: "My goldfish,"
he said,
"are spunky and bright and fast, just like me"
as he flashed away to his fish tank,
his letting us in on it raking our hearts.

1939: The Oedipus Complex

Caroming from side to side
each subway curve
smacked my cousins and me
against passengers, poles and each other
protozoan-stupid.
Mothers yelled
"Stop bumping!"
Our bones stung deliciously.
Mothers were so insistent
we couldn't hear them.
"Let boys be," Aunt Ceil answered for us.

We cartwheeled at Flushing World's Fair,
then rushed the ramps
at the Trylon and Perisphere—
a towering pyramid and a plump globe—
one a weapon to flash, the other softly to touch.
"Which is which?" I asked Aunt Ceil.
I had to know.

Age 6, Freud happens.

Want

From the innermost coil of earth's sanctum
rises heat of done and to be redone,
new stories old, old stories new.
She struggles at bedside in A.M.,
cloths clinging, sexuality strangling her will,
gropes for her slippers and her mind falls out
on herself as unsought, unbecoming, unused,
haunted by memory gap, hunting in sighs.
She's much to do. Makes her toilette, her tea,
discerningly tugs at her dress to conform to her amplitude.
She'd be loved by many if only they'd know her
and to all who don't know her she loves fiercely back
in plump fullness of all she would want it to be.
Post-Its are stuck on the fridge in small purled notations
to accomplish the big things out there for the little things in here.
The notations are pending. Everything's pending,
Tuxedo cat, black and white, who curled 'round her leg, caressing,
doesn't live here anymore, after its beginning, an ending,
a camaraderie, a touching not to recalibrate.
Expectantly, the lady picks up a romance novel,
black words wander across whiteness
looking for where they belonged before her eyes lost them.
On this morning, day-off, shopping day,
the clock grows spacious between marks of minutes,
the day will be measured by price and availability,
by the cost of living to stock her cabinets and closets,
the kitchen and bedroom, the things done and to be redone
in the heat of existence on this windless hot day.

This Man of Several Parts

The traffic stopped for him
as he walked outside the crosswalk,
not meaning to deny the majesty of laws
or make a show of power as he took me by the elbow
to conduct me to the far side;
you'd wonder how we got there
not following rules one mostly does.
He had quick senses, brainwork speeding
the things that keep things moving,
cause stir and fascination in those around him.
Like his mind, his body too was rapid,
too swift, too focused to stop and search out motives
and machinations of the simpler and slower sort,
even those whose treacheries had brought him down.
Unstopped energy cut his wisdom short,
short-circuited extensions of his mind
which catch the wiliness of charlatans
so he, astounded innocent, would be taken by surprise
and attribute it to consequence of fate
(in denial that some men are made that way);
blindsided, yet never disappointed. Optimist,
he took his bearings from the Trinity and goodness
which always seemed enough to see him through.
I, a Jew, would understand his faith.
I wished I had his ingenuousness and fire.
When all is said, I got more from admiring.

The Skater

This is his character.
It is not his doing.
It is not his fault.
It is not his glory.
It is like his love for ice-cream
in a bowl or on a cone or a stick,
unscripted of moral or meaning: a taste
satisfying desire, a spasm of immediacy like mating.
He's a swimmer, and in the winter ice-skates
brilliantly, as though he draws glister from ice
as he flashes past at lake's edge,
as he enters the center to demonstrate.
At sixty he still plays hockey on the frozen lake
and urges boys to clip him, aggrieves them so they must,
then flips them onto their backs so they hate the old man,
wish he'd go back to his home or "wherever he came from."
Summers on beachfront he lives in his splendor,
throws open his arms to the sun, goes it one better
with vigorous swirls of the furled umbrella
digs into the sand, deepening the auger
that's put to the task to shut out the sun
to stake his claims at the picnic party.
You see him, you see him pausing
at the rich flower patch he's planted;
he introduces himself to his new self each day
in massive recognition of what's excellent.
What is a man to do, but be himself?

An Outlier Who Couldn't Be Resisted

Born old line in the old city
A new kind of face, an outlier
Who couldn't be resisted
Or resented for his sweet
Temperament and charm;
Polite and audacious in unique mixture.
Loved at young age by girls in secret rooms
Or rooms where you knew not to enter
Where he touched and she's liked the feel
Because with it came feelings.
His baseball glove, hung on a peg
In his room studded with happiness,
Was the envy of friends for its deep pocket
And perfect Neatsfoot Oil that blackened its palm.
Like all private rooms of intelligent people
His chamber held doubts and on seldom occasions
Quiet moods as he smoked one or two cigarettes.
He was the friend of friends
For his glove and smiling demeanor
And of neighbors, his earnestness
Until one bright sunny day the curly-haired
Handsome young man
Slit his wrists.

His Letter to Her

I bend for the fallen page in innocence.
The emptied dish that was fruit-filled:
a sudden open air, walls gone,
the presence of you
cluttered with remembrances taking their leave:
pandemonium.

Nothing. All the wealth that was and will be
reduced to a personal wish.
Woman, although you're not physically far
your slumber's a saving cloak
transmitting dreams in your flesh:
incorruptibly.

I sever the text
read and unread of each other,
sheets which might fathom your charm,
explain my reluctance;
while you, sleeping, slip into your own shelter:
rid of me.

Bless you, love, in your house without an address,
architecture floating without gravity,
your constituencies changing, lacking me.
If dreams are escape, I submit, lose me
in your imprudent way that has me in mind:
by exclusion.

I bend for the fallen page, my reverie seeks you.
As myths come alive when called up,
so you impinge, a truth become.
Though my senses attempt, my brain snarls:
innocent or not, we cannot be one—
we'd be done for.

Lament in the Garment Loft

(After Shakespeare's Sonnet 30,
"When to the sessions of sweet silent thought")

When to the sweatshop where seersucker suits
slyly pucker to kiss crotches last
zippered in gray gabardines over Fruit
of the Loom, we false-lengthen inseams and short-size the waist
and new wail our woe at our forelady foe
who browbeats us to cheat us the more cheaply we toil;
then hotly I weep I e'er learned to sew
pockets, cuffs, loops, till my coddling tears boil.
Then seize I Yussel and Fu Yi to sign on
to the Trouser Trades Union, open a door
for Pedro, Rosinda, Abdul to latch on
to Croesus's riches . . . or more suitably, more!
     But when my boss notes my sly, puckish trend,
      my long suit's played out and botched britches I mend.

Sales Flight: Departure/Arrival

The scream runway disembowels memory.
Wrappings hold us in.

My future waits so sure
unsure
I do not care.
I am the bull's eye's nimbus.

I pluck any magazine.
Color photos flip by
abstracted as past pursuits and panics.

Sunlight powers through the port.
Stewards' affectations and shadows
alight on my frame.

Again bucking when we pull down.
Little children in the seats ahead shout "We'll make it!"
so worldly-wise with TV-stuffing they are.

This corporate face.
Chuffing crowds and the itchy wools of meetings
that what is next I do not know
though I had practiced it before.

The customer's "Mr. Steinberg?"
Then
quick-talk.

Shaking It Off

This fallow night, a vagrant light illumines
a shadow shape of day's unconscious consciousness:
the waiting stare, a wind that forces sodden leaves
against the window pane telling of summer's
forfeit as though gaiety had not been—
the striped umbrella's wicker wine beneath,
the heedless crash into green waves
and the later shivering tones, "Why yes, it's cold."

Day undergirds this frost I've wakened to.
At dawn, chapel bells charge the air
within the muted grayness of my room;
portents toll to fasten acquiescence
in commandments of the Many and the One.
Come day's toils I'll do what needs be done.

Job Interview

I am the point of origin of three planes
at the bottom corner of this sharp-lit room,
which for you is my point of disappearance
as you stare at me from your desk.
References? His name is Henry and hers is Millie.
> *(They're the bears at my home, like you here in your lair.*
> *They try to grip me, but I roar.)*
Productivity? I keep up with loping antelope, I'm that swift.
> *(You cannot catch me.)*
Multi-task? I range over the Urals and the Great Lakes all at once.
> *(I'm soaring now!)*
What? . . . I prefer a Chevy . . . Oh? . . . so, I'll buy a Lexus,
of course, of course, just like yours!
> *(You can stick cleats to my sides, they won't pierce.)*
Arrested? If I'm guilty for doing nothing, I won't argue.
> *(Whatever.)*
Health? I won't cost you medical coverage,
I have no glands or organs within me,
I am inoperable by physicians
by my family
by myself.
I am boneless, brainless, heartless,
and I don't want to be homeless.
I'll fit in swell here.
> *(Have you an affiliate in Indianapolis?)*
I know who I am.
> *(It's there on your desk in writing.)*
You say the watermark on my resume is
upside-down
so would I please get you a respectable one?

My Photograph

I like to look at this photograph of me,
it's me at my place of work.
I like to just sit here and look at it.
I'm never activated by its stillness,
by what's bundled up in it.
I react against anyone seeing it.
But actually, in it, I'm pretty okay.
Interesting, that my finger's curled on my chin,
as though I'm figuring.
In the photo behind me is a cabinet
that's shut but sometimes slides open
from the slant of things.
It's a Steelcase file cabinet filled
with ambiguities and what gets me nervous
if I open a file.
I or somebody put the papers there,
it could be somebody else's there,
it could be others' turmoils and pitfalls
not mine. But no, the tabs carry my name.
The case doesn't have a lock in it, you see,
it's a cheap cabinet so I don't need a key to open or lock it,
it's all right there for me
no matter how I keep mulling over that
I'd be better employed somewhere else.
But no.
I don't consider myself braggadocio
when I admit I look so darn good
in my photo,
the boss of this Steelcase file cabinet.

~~~~~~~~

Merry girls swing by,
youthful gift of sureness summoning graces,
hopefuls hasting through, light-stepped.

Envoi: Metaphysical Geriatrical

All poets stay newborn;
'tis Spirit lifts their lives along
through chambers inexplicable; wrong
are numbers; for poets' Song
dissolves Time, can make of night, the morn,
and firmament its negligible pawn.

If so, what's Age?
An opportune blank Page.

In Appreciation

I thank my editor and publisher Ellen Foos for her deftness over a period of months in convincing me to put this book together, and for her tact and expertness in helping me see it through to completion. My wife Marcia and Ellen's associate Arlene Weiner also contributed to selecting the poems. My many sessions with the excellent critique groups U.S. 1 Poet's Cooperative, Delaware Valley Poets, and Artsbridge helped me burnish my ideas about how diversely poetry could be "done" and how individual poems could be accomplished.

Publication Credits

A Different Latitude: "The Sunday Travel Section"

Aries (Texas Wesleyan University): "An Overheard War"

Art Times Journal: "Patio Lunch at a Sculpture Garden" and "Love's Losings"

The Aurorean: "Bright Day"

Bucks County Writer: "In the Heat of Bloom" (publ. as "Japan")

Canadian Writers Journal (Canada): "Moon Shining over Sea"

Chaffin Journal (Eastern Kentucky University): "What It's Like to Create Poetry" (publ. as "Other Wise")

Clark Street Review: "Poland before Gdańsk: 2" (publ. as "Poland before Uprising")

Deronda Review (Israel): "Love's Lastings" (publ. as "Epithalamium") and "An Overheard War"

Diner: "A Boy's September Catskill" (publ. as "A Boy's September Song")

Dissections (University of Brighton, England): "Cyclops"

Epicenter: "Poland before Gdańsk: 1" (publ. as "Poland before Gdansk")

Flint Hills Review (Emporia State University): "China"

Lawrence Library Circular: "An Overheard War"

Lucidity (Featured Poet): "In the Harbor" and "New Orleans Parish" (publ. as "By Naval Dock, New Orleans")

The Lyric: "Of Emily Dickinson" (publ. as "To Emily") and "The Sunday Travel Section"

Oatmeal and Poetry: "Pre-Dawn Awakeness"

Parody: "Fixing Her Wagon"

Peeking Cat (England): "Cat Visit—Lawrenceville"

Poems on a Red Oak Branch (New Jersey Poetry Society Anthology): "A
   Woman's Ghost Story" and "Next Stop Next" *(Prizewinner–*publ. as
   "After-Hours Muse")

Poetalk: "A Woman's Ghost Story"

Poets' Paper: "Divorce"

RB's Poets' Viewpoint: "The Sunday Travel Section" *(Award Winner)*

River Oak Review (Elmhurst College): "Calypso Immortal"

U.S.1 Newspaper: "Crossing 7th Avenue" (publ. as "Crossing Nassau
   Street") and "Einstein and Me"

U.S. 1 Worksheets: "An Aesthete Takes the World As It Is" and "Next Stop
   Next" and "Some Rules and Regulations Re: Felines" and "Poland
   before Gdańsk: 1" (publ. as "Poland before Gdansk")

Waterways: "Overload" and "Fine Liquor of Philosophy" and "Divorce"
   (publ. as "Home")

Wild River Review: "Dour Journey" and "Sales Flight: Departure/Arrival"

Wisconsin Review (University of Wisconsin Oshkosh): "Overload"

Writers Gallery: "Patio Lunch at Grounds for Sculpture" and "A Boy's
   September Catskill" and "A Woman's Ghost Story" (publ. as "A
   Peasant Woman's Ghost Story") and "Fine Liquor of Philosophy"
   and "My Master the Authority"

Author's Biography

Harvey Steinberg has been nothing if not busily eclectic. The selection of poems in this book is meant to reflect that temperament. Now 88, he previously satisfied that disposition as National Vice-President of an AFL-CIO industrial union; as Deputy Director of an esteemed urban revitalization program and Executive Director of its Economic Development arm; in politics, as an Assembly District Leader in New York City; and in civic affairs as environmental advocate in New Jersey. In later years he performed freelance journalism alongside his wife Marcia and served as co-founder of a large arts organization in central New Jersey. He has taught in several disciplines, including writing and literature, at colleges and universities in New Jersey and Pennsylvania. His practice of poetry and the visual arts began in early youth, with huge gaps over the course of his life. He holds a B.A. from the City University of New York, where he was editor of the college literary/art magazine, a J.D. from Brooklyn Law School, and has graduate training in several disciplines. He lives in Lawrenceville, New Jersey, with Marcia, a sociologist, and has immediate family in Virginia and Boston. Raised partly in the Catskills and mostly in an old working-class section of Brooklyn, he gives thanks to his father who asked his adolescent son the shattering question, "Harvey, would you want everyone to be like you?"